Anger the Silent Killer

Anger the Silent Killer

The Fire Inside

Dr. Jeffery L. Walker

authorHOUSE®

AuthorHouse™
1663 Liberty Drive
Bloomington, IN 47403
www.authorhouse.com
Phone: 1 (800) 839-8640

Published by AuthorHouse 09/24/2015

ISBN: 978-1-5049-5300-9 (sc)
ISBN: 978-1-5049-5299-6 (e)

Print information available on the last page.

This book is printed on acid-free paper.

Acknowledgments

I would like to give a shout-out to those who empowered me to write this Anger Management Workbook. I extend special thanks to all the individuals who shared their observations of the stresses and strains that they have encountered throughout the course of their lives. All human beings will experience anger, but the key is what are you going to do about it. May this workbook strengthen your intellectual ability so that you can understand the dynamics of anger, step by step. Through this workbook, I hope that I will inspire you to learn how to take anger, anxiety, and frustration and recycle it into cognitive fuel. I give all praise to my supreme being for giving me the courage and strength to complete this Anger Management Workbook.

Dedication

This Anger Management Workbook is dedicated to all the people who are experiencing uncontrollable anger. My ultimate hope is that you will learn the cognitive skills that will prohibit you from psychological and emotional turbulence due to unprocessed anger.

Contents

Introduction

This workbook is designed to assist individuals with Anger Management problems. It consists of eight essential topics that will modify your cognitive and behavioral patterns to where the participant will learn to think before exploding. This workbook can be used in an individual or group setting. The concepts and skills presented in this Anger Management Workbook are best learned through repetition and completing the assignments in a timely manner. When using this eight-step Anger Management Workbook, an individual will learn to develop the skills that are necessary to rise above their cognitive temperament. I strongly encourage you to pay close attention to the vital steps that will enhance your ability to understand your anger style. It will allow you to rid yourself of consequences that will occur when you modulate into a rage... Good luck my friends!

The Biology of Anger

Do you ever wonder how anger can get you in trouble before you know it? It has to do with the way our bodies work and how we perceive internal and external stimuli. For example, someone offends you with derogatory statements, and you react opposed to responding in a healthy manner. From a cognitive perspective, we must all remember that no one can make you mad; you make yourself angry by the way you interpret stimuli. If unresolved anger is left untreated, it can be detrimental to self and others. Anger is the nucleus (center part) of "Domestic Violence" which has woven into the main fabric of society.

The Fire in Side

Anger is often called **"the fire inside,"** is one of our most powerful emotions. It has a dual component because it can become a teaching mechanism or your greatest enemy. There is a biological process that occurs in the brain when people become angry. Anger happens when people are unable to manipulate or control the opposition.

Step 1:

Overview of Your Anger Management

This self-help workbook is designed to help you work through your emotional turbulence. In this first step, you will begin to know and understand the dynamics of your anger. It will include understanding your purpose for change, terms, definitions, myths about anger, and rewards verse consequences. At the conclusion of this first step, you will have a better understanding of how and why you get angry. This step will assist you in navigating through your 8 step program with great success.

I. Purpose of this anger management workbook is to

Acknowledge your anger style.

Not be afraid to be assertive about your feelings.

Get in touch with self and your environment.

Examine your gamut of emotions so you can identify what you feel.

Recognize your psychosocial triggers so that you can release your anger in a healthy manner as soon as possible.

II. Definitions of the AAHRR Components

What is anger?

Anger is a natural emotion that affects all human beings. It ranges from mild irritation to intense fury and rage. Many people are unaware of how to identify what they are feeling. During this step, you will learn the vital terms and definitions that will help you work through this anger management workbook.

Anger: Occurs when an individual cannot control or manipulate a situation. Anger is a very powerful emotion, and if left unmonitored it can be damaging to one's psychological and physical health. Anger has an emotional cousin called **"fear"** and the two emotions work in conjunction with each other.

1

Aggression: On the other hand, can be intimidating or cause bodily harm to another person or property. Aggression has an emotional cousin called **"passive aggressive behavior."** It occurs when another individual is mad at you when you are not around. They may do something that affects you indirectly such as; damage your property, bring bodily harm to a close friend, family member or publicize negative information about you.

Hostility: Refers to a set of attitudes and judgments' that fuels aggressive behaviors.

Resentment: This occurs when an individual is **passive** and allows their anger to simmer and chooses to do nothing about it, which will eventually cause an "emotional eruption."

Rage: Is the apex (top) of your anger, which consists of two primary components. "Cognitive Movement and Physical Altercation." **Cognitive Movement** occurs when an individual is thinking about what they are going to do to someone if they do not stop bothering them. **Physical Altercation** occurs when an individual can no longer tolerate the behavior of the opposition and explode into **"rage"** which is also known as **"temporary insanity"** which has a duration of **"7 seconds."**

- Prior to learning the definitions of the AAHRR components, did you ever confuse them? Circle Yes or No.

III. When does anger become unmanageable?

Anger becomes a problem when it overpowers your ability to use logical thinking. When your anger feels too intense and happens repetitiously, you are in definite trouble. Once this occurs, your body is in "checkmate" (unable to move). Anger has a direct effect on your holistic make-up.

- List some ways anger may be affecting you physically.

_____

_____

_____

_____

IV. Reward Vs. Consequences

The expression of anger initially has two components (e.g., releasing tension, and controlling something or someone). Anger can be one of your greatest educators, but it can also be your greatest enemy. When the consequence is greater than the reward, then don't do it. To the contrary, when the reward is greater than the consequence the outcome is brighter.

- List some ways that anger was more of a **reward** and educated you.

_____

_____

_____

_____

- List some **consequences** that occurred when you inappropriately expressed your anger.

_____

_____

_____

_____

V. What role does mythical thinking play about anger?

Most people do not realize that anger is a learned behavior. Anger is a natural emotion that is elicited by either internal or external stimuli, meaning something that causes activity.

Below are some myths about anger.

Myth1: **Anger is genetically inherited,** not true. Research studies show that the expression of anger is a learned behavior; therefore this behavior can be modified to express your anger in appropriate ways.

Myth 2: **Anger always leads to aggression,** not true. The escalation of anger can be controlled by learning how to de-escalate your cognitive process (thought patterns).

Myth 3: **If you are aggressive you will get what you want,** not true. The ultimate goal of aggression is to dominate and control, whereas, assertiveness is when you stand up for what you believe.

Myth 4: **Releasing your anger by any means necessary,** not good. Research studies have found, however, that people who vent their anger in an aggressive manner tend to reinforce their anger.

- Before our discussion, did you believe in any of the above myths? Circle Yes or No and explain one of your myths.

_____

_____

_____

_____

VI. Do you become angry on a regular basis?

Expressing your anger can become routine assignment and create a negative response to stimuli. What this entails is that you will automatically in a repetitious manner, display maladaptive (bad) behavior that will consistently result in negative consequences.

- Is anger a habit for you? Circle Yes or No.

_____

_____

_____

- Has your anger created consequences for you? Circle Yes or No.

_____

_____

_____

_____

VII. Breaking the Cycle of Your Anger

You can modify your behavior by being aware of your psychosocial triggers, which are things that cause you to become angry.

- List some anger management strategies that you used in the past.

_____

_____

_____

_____

VIII. How to Use Your Anger Meter and Determine the Level of Your Anger

Monitor your anger by using the anger meter scale below. If you score 1 to 3 on the anger meter, this usually indicates that you are relatively calm. However, if you score 4 to 7 on the anger meter this means that you are beginning to explode, and if you score 8 to 10 you have lost control and in a state of rage. Between the levels from 1 to 7 you have a chance to control your anger before it leads to negative consequences but when you reach the level of 8 to 10, consequences are inevitable. Below, monitor and record your highest anger level throughout the course of 1 week.

_____M _____ T _____ W _____ Th _____ F _____ Sa _____ Sun

Anger Meter

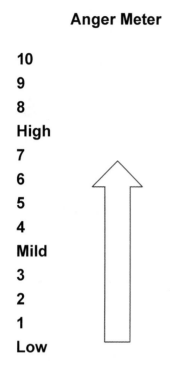

10

9

8

High

7

6

5

4

Mild

3

2

1

Low

Now that you understand a little bit more about your anger, you are well on your way to understanding why you get angry.

What did you learn from Step 1?

_____

_____

_____

_____

_____

_____

_____

_____

_____

_____

_____

_____

_____

_____

_____

_____

_____

_____

_____

_____

_____

Do not rely on short-term memory; always refer to your notes.

Step 2:

The Manifestation of Anger

In this step, you will start to analyze your anger. This step will help you identify various events that cause your anger to escalate.

I. Psychosocial Triggers

Triggers are also known as a stimulus that causes activity. There are two types of triggers, external and internal.

External: These are things that are done to us. For example; someone lying about you or putting you down.

Internal: These are messages we give ourselves called negative self-talk. This type of internal stimuli rather it is past or present can cause you to get angry.

People usually get angry when they encounter negative events, but often their anger can also stem from past events. Here are examples of scenarios that can trigger anger:

- Having money or property stolen from you.

- Being accused of something that you didn't do.

- A girl/boyfriend leaving you for another person.

- Being ridiculed or put down by friends or family members.

- Being caught up in long traffic lines.

- Waiting too long at the doctor's office.

- A family member or friend is not paying back money owed to you.

Write down some of the things that trigger your anger, these are called red flags.

_____

_____

_____

_____

II. Anger Cues: Four major categories

Let's examine the four major cues. Before anger is full-blown, there are indicators that are consistent with the progression of anger. These cues will serve as your warning signs to let you know that you are having a biological reaction to anger. There are four warning categories: physical, behavioral, emotional, and cognitive (thought process). In each category list the cues that you experience when you get angry.

1) **Physical Cues** – Your body has a natural response to anger stimuli such as; increase heart rate, increase respiration, dry mouth, and hot flashes. List some ways in which your body physically tells you that you are getting angry.

_____

_____

_____

_____

_____

2) **Behavioral Cues** – Things you do with your body such as; clench your teeth or fist, elevate your voice in a threatening manner or mean mug a person (staring at them).

List some of the ways your behavioral characteristics surface when you get angry.

_____

_____

_____

_____

3) Emotional Cues – Often other feelings work in concert with anger; e.g., fear, hurt, disappointment, resentment, jealousy. List some other secondary emotions that you may exhibit when you get angry.

_____

_____

_____

_____

4) Cognitive Cues – Things that you think about when you are getting angry; e.g., revenge, being aggressive with someone, using derogatory statements to give the impression that you want to do bodily harm to someone. List some of your negative self-talk that you use to activate your anger.

_____

_____

_____

_____

III. How Are You Doing With Monitoring Your Anger?

In this session, you will start to record your behavioral characteristics and identify various scenarios that cause your anger to ascend. From this point on you will monitor every step you take and every move you make until you have a firm grip on your anger triggers. When monitoring your anger on a weekly basis, you will begin through second nature to notice right away your psychosocial triggers, the four cues that your body will inform you that you are escalating. In the next session, you will learn to apply the appropriate strategy to defuse your anger in a healthy manner.

1) Go back to Step 1 and look at the anger meter and write down the number that you reached during the past week. _____

2) Do you remember what caused your anger?

_____

_____

_____

_____

3) Go back to Step 2 and re-examine the four cues and explain which one you experienced or if you witness all four cues.

Physical cues _____

Behavioral cues _____

Emotional cues _____

Cognitive cues _____

IV. Verbal and Non-verbal Triggers

Verbal and non-verbal triggers are the fuel for your anger. "Perception" is the key phase of anger management. The environment is not stressful it is how we perceive it. Therefore, it is vital that you understand how thoughts, feelings and behavior originate. In anger management, you want to focus on two types of stimuli, visual and auditoria. Visual is when you see something that arouses your anger, whereas, auditoria is when you hear something that elicits your anger. Here are some basic psych 101 facts that are crucial to understanding how your anger manifests.

First of all, thoughts produce feelings, and feelings produce behavior, and behaviors produce either a reward or consequence. So, what produce thoughts? The way that you see or hear something is called "perception" which shapes your thoughts. Let's examine some common verbal triggers that can provoke your anger.

- criticism

- blaming

- teasing

- profanity

List some verbal encounters that you had that made you angry.

_____

_____

_____

_____

Now let's examine some nonverbal triggers that have the potential to raise your anger level.

- Sighing

- Mocking

- Throwing or kicking objects

- Grimacing, sneering, or frowning

List some nonverbal encounters that you had that made you angry.

_____

_____

_____

_____

V. The Blueprint for rage

Anger is the pilot light for rage because unresolved **anger** turns into **resentment,** and unresolved resentment turns into **rage.** Rage has two components: **cognitive movement** and **physical altercation.** The cognitive form of rage occurs when you are thinking about doing great bodily harm to someone. By the same token, a physical altercation occurs when you act on whatever it is that you are thinking about doing to someone. A physical altercation is very dangerous because the consequence is greater than the reward. When you are caught up in your rage, the judicial system calls this "temporary insanity" which can have a duration of 7 seconds. Immediately after you reach the level of rage you will move into what I call the **"quiet storm."** It is the last phase of rage and during this phase you will feel **guilt** and **shame** because of your explosive behavior. Also during this phase you do not want to talk or to be around anyone and that is why you will say to someone who is trying to calm you down to just **"leave me alone."**

Write a blueprint of your rage by following the above scenario of anger, resentment and rage (ARR).

_____

_____

_____

_____

VI. The Ouch Theory!

You hurt me!

O = observation, what did you see or hear.

U = unexplainable, do you know why it happen.

C = control, you are angry because you could not control the situation.

H = hurt, you are hurt because your moral system was attacked.

People say offensive things to one another to dethrone them and make them feel like they are useless to self and society. When this occurs, it is important that you apply the **"ouch theory."** Once you learn to defuse someone who is trying to belittle you, you can take their power away without confrontation.

Once you understand the dynamics of anger, you can alleviate or at best mitigate the powers of misguided anger. Please remember that anger cannot grow if you are

an assertive person (stand up for what you believe in). However, if you are a passive person (hold everything inward) anger can grow. At the initial contact with your anger stimuli, be assertive in a healthy manner towards the person that you are angry at, and tell that person how you feel. This type of assertiveness will block the growth of your anger because you do not allow your anger to simmer.

Therefore, you will block your level of rage. Remember that the **ego** and **pride** are extremely sensitive to anger stimuli so; I strongly encourage you to practice your ARR format because this blueprint is accurate in terms of stopping the manifestation of your anger.

Great job you are getting there!

What did you learn from Step 2?

_____

_____

_____

_____

_____

_____

_____

_____

_____

_____

_____

_____

_____

_____

_____

_____

_____

_____

_____

_____

_____

Do not rely on short-term memory; always refer to your notes.

Step 3:

Strategies That You Can Use to Combat Your Anger

This step is very crucial because you will learn defense mechanism that will assist you in dethroning your anger. In step 1 and 2, you learned about your anger and how anger can control you if you let it. Remember that anger does not have any power but you give it power by not knowing about the biology of anger. In this step, you will learn immediate and preventive strategies. **Immediate** strategies consist of using effective timeouts, relaxation techniques, and the thought stopping technique. **Preventive** strategies consist of cognitive aerobics (exercising your brain so that you can effectively change your irrational beliefs). Lastly, you need to be able to differentiate between a reaction and response. When you **"react"** it does not require cognitive movement (you do not think). However, when you **"respond"** it requires cognitive movement (you think about what you are going to do). When you react to outside stimuli, you will most likely experience a consequence, but when you respond to outside stimuli, you will usually receive a reward.

Are you ready to build a defense for your untamed anger?

I. Controlling Your Ager Before it Controls You

The TSC Format

Think about it? Like other emotions, anger is accompanied by physiological and biological changes in the body. When you get angry, your heart rate and blood pressure will go up, and when this happens in repetition, you can develop serious health problems. Do you want this to happen to you? If not, then pay close attention to the steps in reducing the chance of you becoming a product of anger mismanagement and remember, that anger is not the **"boss"** you are.

There are three primary steps that you must acknowledge in your defense towards your anger. When you are experiencing anger, **the first step is to find the "target"** meaning who or what made you angry.

Your second step is to find the "source" of your anger meaning, why are you angry. **Your third step is to ask yourself "can you change the situation?"** If you cannot

then do not give it power. On the other hand, if you can change the situation, then find a healthy solution through logical thinking. For this cognitive process to work, you must use repetition. Remember that practice do not make you perfect because nothing is perfect. Practice can only make you better and you can always better your best. **Now!!! Practice, practice and practice the above TSC format** because repetition brings proficiency, meaning the more you do something you become highly skilled at it.

Write a time when you got angry and applied the "TSC format."

_____

_____

_____

_____

II. Anger Reduction Plans

Thought Stopping Technique

You will need to close your eyes and picture a stop sign in your mind, telling you to stop whenever you are experiencing unwanted thoughts.

Timeouts

The timeout technique is extremely effective in slowing down the manifestation of your anger. Typically two things happen when people get angry, they usually will become aggressive or go into the passive mold. This particular step in your workbook concentrates on mitigating your anger by blocking it off before it reaches level 10 on your "anger meter". This step also gives you the opportunity to develop some strategies that will help you control your anger.

Every human being should use the timeout strategy when dealing with conflict. The problem with this concept is that we are not taught during our developmental stages how to appropriately use the "timeout method." This method of anger control is very common in anger management. Taking a timeout when confronted with anger is a healthy decision because it takes you away from the source of your anger and allows you to think before you get into a cognitive or physical altercation with someone.

It is a fact that when you use your timeout method as necessary you can prevent yourself from reaching level 10 on the anger meter.

Another effective timeout method is to go for a walk, call a friend or family member and talk with them so that you can release your tension. When would you use your timeout strategy?

_____

_____

_____

_____

Relaxation Techniques

When experiencing anger the first thing that you want to do is find a quiet place to sit or lie down. If it is not physically possible to find that quiet place, you can still utilize your relaxation techniques. After finding that quiet place you can began to scan your body for stress. To better manage stress, you must first recognize how and when tension is affecting you. By learning to scan your body for stress, you will learn how to become more aware of those situations that trigger anger in you. Below are strategies that you can use to stay calm and cool.

➢ Begin by paying attention to your feet and legs. Start by wiggling your toes, and then rotate your feet and relax them.

➢ Now focus on your lower torso. Become aware of any tension or pain in your lower back. Relax as fully as possible. Notice any tension in your hips, pelvic area, or buttocks. Relax these areas.

➢ Move the focus to your diaphragm and stomach. Take a couple of slow deep breaths. Feel yourself relaxing, more and more deeply.

➢ Focus on your breathing and your chest area. Search for any tension here. Take a few slower breaths, and then a few deep breaths, and let go of any tension.

➢ Next, pay attention to your shoulders, neck, and throat. Swallow a couple of times and notice any tension or soreness in your throat and neck. Rotate your head clockwise a few times. Now reverse and rotate your head the other way. Shrug your shoulders, noting any tension and then relax.

➢ Begin at the top of your head and scan for tension. Look for pain in your forehead. Perhaps there is a band of pain around your head. Maybe there is pain or tension

35

behind your eyes. Notice any tightness in your jaw. Check for locking or grinding of teeth and taut lips. Be aware of your ears. Go back over your head and relax each part.

➢ Now re-scan your entire body for any remaining tension. Allow yourself to relax more and more deeply. I recommend doing this exercise every day for a few weeks until you have a good idea of where your body holds tension. It is a good idea to do these exercises at work, in between tasks, and when you return home at the end of the day. It is also a good idea to keep a diary each day of the location where the tension seems to concentrate and whether you experience angry feelings or felt upset. At the end of each week, go back and read your diary, this will help you come to terms with what you are experiencing. Remember that this body scanning technique can be used in any situation (Johnson, 1999).

Balance Breathing

Another way to mitigate your stress level is through using appropriate breathing techniques. Proper breathing is one of the most natural antidotes for stress, and yet most people take breathing for granted. To live a healthy life, you have to breathe. Deep breathing is one of the ways that the body stimulates the lymphatic system, which helps remove waste from the body. In fact, deep breathing is the only way the lymphatic system is turn on to perform the vital function of removing cellular waste from throughout the body. Below are some effective ways to secure the "breath of life".

➢ Lie down on a blanket or rug on the floor. Bend your knees and place your feet about eight inches apart, with your toes turned slightly outward. Make sure that your spine is straight.

➢ Scan your body for tension and release any that you note.

➢ Place your left hand on your stomach and your right hand on your chest.

➢ Inhale slowly and deeply through your nose, filling your abdomen. Push the air down to your belly. Notice your left hand being pushed up. Your chest should move only a little underneath your right hand and only with your abdomen.

➢ Now inhale through your nose and exhale through your nose. Your mouth, tongue, and jaw will be relaxed. Take long, slow breaths and raise and lower your abdomen. Close your eyes and focus on your breathing as you become more and more relaxed.

➤ Continue this breathing exercise for about five or ten minutes. Do this once or twice a day.

➤ At the end of each deep breathing session, take a moment or two to scan your body for tension. Compare the tension you feel at the end of the exercise with what you experienced when you began (Johnson, 1999).

Even though you were instructed to do this exercise lying down, the basic technique may be practiced in a sitting or standing position.

Meditation

Meditation is an effective way to cope with stress. I strongly encourage everyone to meditate at the end of the day because meditation is an excellent way to clear your cognitive pathways. Meditation is used throughout the world and is particularly useful for achieving deep relaxation and reducing stress. Use these steps below to navigate through your meditation. Wait for about one month before you evaluate the results.

➤ Go to a quiet place and assume the posture of your choice. Scan your body for tension and relax. Close your eyes and become aware of your breathing. Breathe through your nose. Inhale, exhale, and then pause. Allow yourself to breathe in an easy and natural way.

➤ As you inhale, say the word so to yourself. Continue to breathe out and say the word hum to yourself. Continue breathing in and out, repeating so as you inhale and hum as you exhale.

➤ When thoughts or perceptions threaten to take your attention away from your breathing, let go of them quickly and return to saying so as you inhale and hum as you exhale. Continue this for twenty minutes.

➤ After you complete the exercise, spend a few minutes resting with your eyes closed. Allow yourself to experience your thoughts and feelings. Take the time to appreciate the calming effects of the meditation before returning to your activities (Johnson, 1999).

NOTE: You will be very surprised of the calming effect that meditation will bring to you.

What did you learn from Step 3?

_____

_____

_____

_____

_____

_____

_____

_____

_____

_____

_____

_____

_____

_____

_____

_____

_____

_____

_____

_____

_____

_____

Do not rely on short-term memory; always refer to your notes.

Step 4:

What Is Your Anger Style?

Thus far, you have been practicing on understanding the origin of your anger, but you do not know what style of anger that you represent. This step will help you determine your anger style.

I. The Six Towers of Anger

➤ **The Blamer**: This anger style blames everyone else for their shortcomings.

➤ **The Exploder:** This person likes to simmer and lets everything build up inside of them before they experience an "emotional eruption", (explode).

➤ **The Put Downer**: Will always find a great need to dethrone someone to make them feel better by saying hurtful things about someone else.

➤ **The Stuffer**: Have similar characteristics of the exploder except "The Stuffer" will hold everything in and pretends like nothing is wrong.

➤ **The Triangulator:** gossips a lot and try to get everyone around him/her to co-sign for their biddy (gossipy) behavior.

➤ **The Withdrawer:** This person will pull out of a situation and allow their anger to develop in solitude.

Now that you are aware of the different anger styles, which style do you represent? Give an example.

_____

_____

_____

_____

List a name of a person in your life that fit each profile.

Blamer _____

Exploder _____

Put Downer _____

Stuffer _____

Triangulator_____

Withdrawal _____

For the next seven days, write down your anger style. It will help you tune in with the dynamics of your anger.

Monday _____

Tuesday _____

Wednesday _____

Thursday _____

Friday _____

Saturday _____

Sunday _____

II. Laughter Can Do Wonders For Distressing Your Anger

Throughout history, there have been reports that a positive attitude and laughter have improved the health of individuals with chronic illnesses. Research studies have also showed that laughter is very effective in diminishing stress by focusing on the "funny side of life." If you can learn to implement laughter in your daily schedule, you would be amazed at how you feel. Make a conscious effort to laugh every day especially if you are feeling a tremendous amount of stress. If there is nothing currently funny to you, then I suggest that you think of a past event that was humorous to you. Re-live that scenario and laugh as hard as you can because laughter is one of the best medicines for stress reduction.

What did you learn from Step 4?

_____

_____

_____

_____

_____

_____

_____

_____

_____

_____

_____

_____

_____

_____

_____

_____

_____

_____

_____

_____

_____

_____

Do not rely on short-term memory; always refer to your notes

Step 5:

The Cycle of Aggression

In this step, you will gain more insight towards aggression that is the action of your anger.

I. The Aggression Cycle

There are three phases of aggression: escalation, explosion, and consequence. These three phases work together to make up the aggression cycle.

Escalation Phase

The escalation phase occurs when your anger triggers are activated. Remember in

Step 2, you learned about your psychosocial stressors and how to monitor them. Your triggers are cues that let you know that you are beginning to escalate. The first phase of the "aggression cycle" is crucial because if you do not block it you will enter the "rage phase" which can have devastating outcomes.

Explosion Phase

The explosion phase is characterized by violence. When you reach this phase you are in trouble. Most people reach this phase because they do not have the cognitive skills to de-escalate the manifestation of their anger. When you reach this aggression phase, the consequence is greater than the reward.

Consequence phase

This phase is the aftermath of the escalation and explosion phase. It is emotionally damaging because you are faced with serious ramifications. However, this is a very painful phase because you will re-live your negative actions.

III. Characteristics of each aggression phase

- In the **escalation phase** you will experience the following behaviors; negative self-talk, hostile behavior, threatening body language, and intense anger.

- In the **explosive phase,** you will show violence, intimidation, linguistic aggression, and destruction.

- In the **consequence phase** you will think about your actions and experience the following; possible jail sentence, guilt and shame, loss of job, loss of friends, and financial costs, or perhaps your life.

Write down a personal scenario of the three aggression phases.

Escalation Phase, what were you thinking?

_____

_____

_____

_____

Explosion Phase, what did you do?

_____

_____

_____

_____

Consequence Phase, what was the outcome?

_____

_____

_____

_____

- Remember that each aggression phase has a direct correlation to your anger meter in Step 2.

What did you learn from Step 5?

_____

_____

_____

_____

_____

_____

_____

_____

_____

_____

_____

_____

_____

_____

_____

_____

_____

_____

_____

_____

_____

Do not rely on short-term memory; always refer to your notes

Step 6:

Review Steps 1, 2, 3, 4, and 5

In this step, you are advised to go back and review Steps 1, 2, 3, 4, and 5. By reviewing these steps, it will help you modify your cognitive process because repetition brings about proficiency. The more you do something you become highly skilled at it, therefore, applying the tools to defuse your anger becomes second nature. Remember that practice does not make you perfect because nothing is perfect, but practice can make you better and you can always better your best.

I. Reviewing Step 1

Define the following terms and remember that these terms are crucial to understanding the manifestation of anger.

Anger

_____

_____

_____

_____

Hostility

_____

_____

_____

_____

Aggression

_____

_____

_____

_____

Passive aggressive

_____

_____

_____

_____

Resentment

_____

_____

_____

_____

Rage

_____

_____

_____

_____

Cognitive Movement

_____

_____

_____

_____

Physical Altercation

_____

_____

_____

_____

Write about one way anger is affecting you.

_____

_____

_____

_____

What is meant by reward verse consequence?

_____

_____

_____

_____

Name two myths about anger?

_____

_____

_____

_____

How often do you get angry? Please circle your answer?

Sometimes / often / all the time

When you were doing Step 1 where did you register on the anger meter? Circle your level. Low / Mild / High

What is your anger strategy? _____

_____

_____

_____

_____

Now that you have completed **Step 1** continue to strive to be the best that you can be. Job well done!

II. Reviewing Step 2

What is meant by psychosocial triggers? _____

_____

_____

_____

_____

What do external stimuli mean?

_____

_____

_____

_____

What do internal stimuli mean?

_____

_____

_____

_____

Name the four anger cues.

_____

_____

_____

_____

Name two verbal triggers.

_____

_____

_____

_____

Name two nonverbal triggers.

_____

_____

_____

_____

Explain the process of rage from beginning to end.

_____

_____

_____

_____

Congratulations on Step 2 because this is a difficult step, and you did it.

III. Reviewing Step 3

Strategies that you can use to combat your anger

What are the four strategies mentioned in Step 3?

1. _____

2. _____

3. _____

4. _____

Are you starting to put it all together now? If so, great job!

IV. Reviewing Step 4

What is your anger style?

Write down the six towers of anger.

1. _____
2. _____
3. _____
4. _____
5. _____
6. _____

Which anger style are you?

_____

Now you know what style of anger you show. You're getting there!

V. Reviewing Step 5

The cycle of aggression

What are the three phases of aggression?

I   _____

II   _____

III _____

You have successfully reviewed the first five steps, but to master these steps, you have to practice, practice, and practice.

What did you learn from Step 6?

_____

_____

_____

_____

_____

_____

_____

_____

_____

_____

_____

_____

_____

_____

_____

_____

_____

_____

_____

_____

_____

_____

Do not rely on short-term memory; always refer to your notes.

Step 7:

Perception

In this step, you will learn about human perception and how it can provoke anger. The things that you hear and see can be misleading if it is geared towards you. How you perceive things is crucial to your cognitive process because thoughts produce feelings and feelings will dictate behavior. Therefore, it is important to check incoming stimuli for clarity (how clear it is) and verity (how truthful it is) before you respond.

I. Auditoria (hear)

People have a high propensity to react to something that they thought they heard, however, this form of perception can be easily manipulated if you do not have a keen awareness. Have you ever thought that you heard something about you, and you reacted in a negative manner? Write down a time when you thought you heard something derogatory about you but later found that to be untrue.

_____

_____

_____

_____

II. Visual (see)

How many times have you thought you saw something and reacted to it but later found out that what you saw was unclear? Write down a scenario where you became angry and why?

_____

_____

_____

_____

Auditoria and visual perception are the two senses that human beings can sometimes misconstrue, and if it is something negative, people tend to act on the assumption, which can bring serious consequences. In full detail write down a time when you experienced a consequence that was based on assumption.

_____

_____

_____

_____

III. Introversion, extraversion, and ambi-version

An **introvert** is a reserved or shy person. This personality trait is more prone to allow their anger to simmer, but can resurrect with a vengeance.

An **extrovert** is a gregarious (social) and unreserved person. This personality trait is very outgoing and more apt to confront.

An **ambivert** is an individual who can oscillate between introversion and extroversion depending on the environment.

These three social traits are essential in your socialization process because they can predict how you process your anger. Write down what social style you have and what your socialization process consists of, in other words, how do you mingle?

_____

_____

_____

_____

Congratulations, you are progressing.

What did you learn from Step 7?

_____

_____

_____

_____

_____

_____

_____

_____

_____

_____

_____

_____

_____

_____

_____

_____

_____

_____

_____

_____

_____

_____

Do not rely on short-term memory; always refer to your notes.

Step 8

Final Call for Change

What was taught to you about anger in the nest (home environment)?

In this step, you will learn how and what you were taught about anger in your family system. All human beings are products of their home environment. Prescription for change is necessary. It is your final step to conquering your anger.

I. Parental Ignorance

Parental Ignorance probably sounds inflammatory, but that is not how it is meant. Instead, it means that parents often are unknowledgeable about shaping the morals, values, and belief system of their children to accommodate the by-laws of society. Ignorance applies to everyone when you lack certain intellectual properties. Parents are more prone to teach their children what they were taught during their developmental stages, and this can be very damaging if the information is incorrect. One of the greatest emotions that human beings tend to run from is the godfather of emotions called **"anger."** Technically, we are afraid of anger primarily because we have not been taught how to deal with it. In society, we are programmed not to show anger because we see anger as a diabolical mindset, when in fact, anger is a natural emotion with a dual impact. Meaning it can be your greatest enemy or your greatest educator. Children should be educated about anger at an early age so that when they reach adulthood they will be able to eliminate the fear of "anger."

Anger is one of the greatest emotional oppositions that we faced. However, through proper education we can learn to understand where it comes from, how it manifest within, and how to alleviate or at best mitigate it.

The problem is that we lack educational skills that will assist us in dethroning our anger. In this step, it is paramount that you think about what messages that you received from your parents in the nest (home) about anger. Keep in mind that most of us were prohibited from showing anger, so we learned through parental programming to block that emotion and substitute it with another less intense emotion. The problem with this form of classical conditioning is the fact that we will most likely experience

what I call "emotional decay" (meaning when one emotion is left untreated the other emotions will become affected). Parents should educate themselves about anger so that they can teach their children healthy ways to express their anger without a physical altercation.

Write down what you were taught about anger during your developmental stages.

_____

_____

_____

_____

Were you allowed to express your anger in your household? If so, what was the outcome?

_____

_____

_____

_____

When you showed anger, how did your parent(s) respond?

_____

_____

_____

_____

When you got angry in school what did your teacher tell you about acting out your anger?

_____

_____

_____

_____

Did your parents punish you for showing your anger?

_____

_____

_____

_____

Today, how do you show your anger?

_____

_____

_____

_____

The bottom line is, when anger is not blocked we will experience "emotional eruption" meaning, we are more apt to explode without intervention.

II. Go back and re-examine Steps 6, 7and 8?

III. Closing Exercise

What have you learned about Anger Management?

_____

_____

_____

_____

_____

List the strategies that you will use to manage your anger.

_____

_____

_____

_____

_____

Are there any specific areas that need improvement?

_____

_____

_____

_____

_____

➢ Do you honestly want to change your cognitive process? Circle Yes or No.

➢ Write a letter to someone that you have hurt by showing inappropriate anger.

Congratulations on completing your Anger Management training!

You Are Now In Charge Of Your Anger, So Go In Peace And Not Pieces.

ONE LOVE!!!

Thank you

Dr. Jeffery L. Walker

Selected Reference

Caring for myself (2010). *Lesson 4: Managing anger.* Retrieved May 21, 2010, from http://www.fcs.msue.msu.edu.

Irving, M. (2008). Cultural identification and academic achievement among African American males. *Journal of Advanced Academics* 19, 676-698.

Johnson, Ernest H. (1999). *Brothers on the mend: understanding and healing male anger for African-American men and women.* Ernest H. Johnson.

July II, W. (1999). *Understanding the tin man: Why so many men avoid intimacy.* New New York: Double Day.

Microsoft Office Professional. (2007). Microsoft Office Online ClipArt/Bing selected Images and graphics. Richmond, WA: Microsoft Corporation One Microsoft Way.

Pearson, Y. (2001). *Anger management youth life skills.* Center City Minnesota Hazelden.

Reilly P.M., Shopshire M.S., Durazzo T.C., and Campbell T.A. *Anger management for substance abuse and mental health clients: Participant workbook.* DHHS Pub. No. (SMA) 03-3817. Rockville, MD. Center for Substance Abuse Treatment, Substance Abuse and Mental Health Services Administration, reprinted 2003.

Stanton, C. (2006). *Life coach in a box.* San Francisco, CA, USA: Chronical Books

U. S. Department of Health and Human Services. Substance Abuse and Mental Health Services Administration Center for Substance Abuse Treatment. 1 Choke Cherry Road, Rockville, MD 20857.

Walker, J. & Harper, H. (2010). *African American males/females why are you so Angry?* Omaha, NE: P.T.C.E Inc.

William Dr., C. C. (1995). US Socioeconomic and racial differences in health: Patterns and explanations. *Ann Rev Sociology* 21, 349-386.

Printed in the United States
By Bookmasters